M O R E
Creative
Sewing

edited by Nancy
Fiedler

TECHNIQUES
by Machine

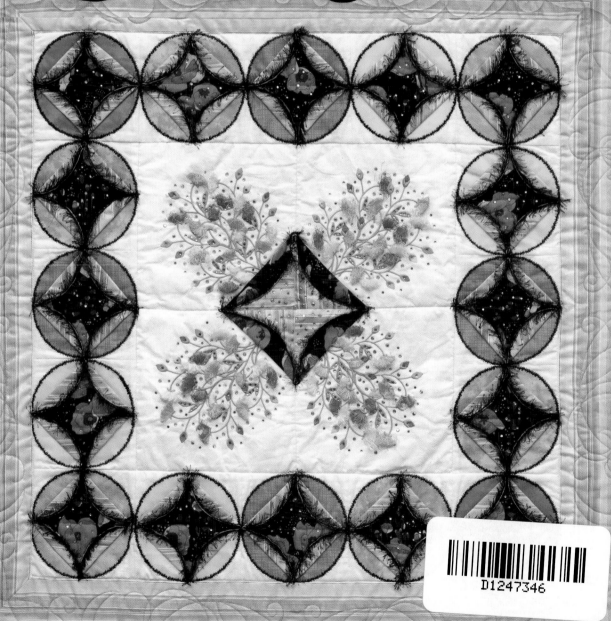

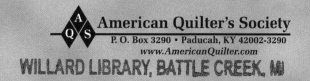

American Quilter's Society
P. O. Box 3290 • Paducah, KY 42002-3290
www.AmericanQuilter.com

Located in Paducah, Kentucky, the American Quilter's Society (AQS) is dedicated to promoting the accomplishments of today's quilters. Through its publications and events, AQS strives to honor today's quiltmakers and their work and to inspire future creativity and innovation in quiltmaking.

Executive Editor: Andi Milam Reynolds
Graphic Design: Lynda Smith
Cover Design: Michael Buckingham
Photography: Charles R. Lynch

Additional copies of this book may be ordered from the American Quilter's Society, PO Box 3290, Paducah, KY 42002-3290, or online at www.AmericanQuilter.com.

Text © 2012 Nancy Fiedler, Editor
Artwork © 2012 American Quilter's Society

Library of Congress Cataloging-in-Publication Data.

Fiedler, Nancy, 1950-
  More creative sewing techniques by machine / by Nancy Fiedler.
    p. cm.
  Includes index.
  Summary: "Learn how sewing machine attachments enable techniques to create quilts and home dec projects. Learn 15 sewing machine techniques, create 10 quilt and home dec projects, and use multiple techniques per project. Supply lists include machine accessories for any brand of machine"--Provided by publisher.
  ISBN 978-1-60460-017-9
  1. Quilting--Patterns. 2. Machine sewing. I. Title.
  TT835.F524 2012
  746.46--dc23
                    2011048030

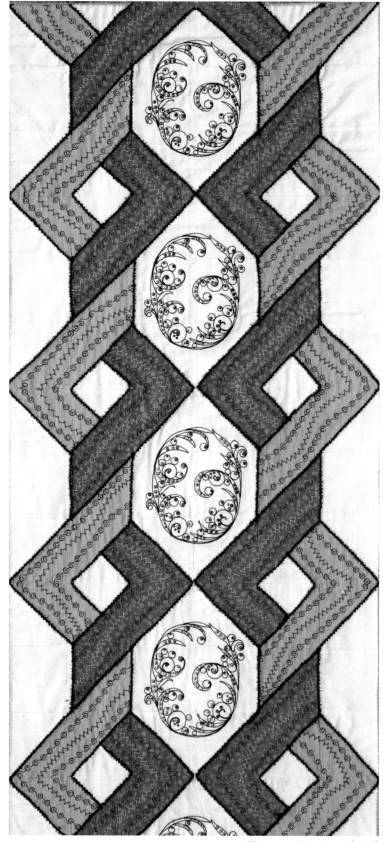

American Quilter's Society
P. O. Box 3290 • Paducah, KY 42002-3290
www.AmericanQuilter.com

Proudly printed and bound in the United States of America

Twisted Ribbon, detail.
Full quilt on page 55.

Title Page: Fringe Fantasy,
page 31.

Contents

Contributors

Kathy Bond – Kathy began sewing doll clothes with her mother. As she grew, she moved on to make clothing for herself. Sewing has been a huge part of her life ever since, whether it's creating gowns, sportswear, draperies, children's clothes, or quilts of every stripe and style. She enjoys teaching as much as the sewing, which has led to ten years as a national educator.

Louis Carney –Louis began his sewing career at the age of 12 in his hometown of Kansas City, Missouri, where he studied tailoring, design, and visual merchandising. He has taught in all 50 states and Mexico and lectured in London. Longarm quilting is his latest venture; he focuses on design and detail elements. A New York City resident, Louis joined the Janome Education Department in 2008.

Nancy Fiedler – A Janome Educational Coordinator, Nancy has been teaching sewing techniques for over 20 years. A regular contributor to Janome Digest and www.Janome. com since 1996, she joined the Janome Education Department in 2004. She specializes in embellishment techniques utilizing the features and accessories of Janome sewing machines, embroidery machines, and sergers. She writes and designs in her studio in Dwight, Illinois.

Valora Hammond –Valora joined Janome America in 2002. She started sewing when she was eight years old. She has been doing custom sewing since she was in high school, expanding to creating garments for contests, stage, and special occasions. She loves to share her passion and enthusiasm in a classroom setting, allowing the consumer a chance to grow with their art. She lives in Denver.

LuAnne Hartley – From Welcome, North Carolina, LuAnne has been in the sewing industry for over 28 years and has a unique knowledge of fabric behavior. While she enjoys quilting, she is a fabric embellisher at heart and often combines free-motion machine embroidery, heirloom sewing, quilting, and garment construction with stunning results. LuAnne's projects are examples of how to get the most from your machine accessories.

Kim Schultz – Kim grew up in New Orleans and began her sewing journey at the age of eight when her mother taught her how to sew. She loves garment construction and home dec sewing and made her first quilt in 1999; she's been hooked ever since. She began her career with Janome as a freelance educator in 2008, traveling from her home in Slidell, Louisiana.

Elaine Yingling – Elaine has created original designs for wearable art; accessories; quilts; embroidery; and performance wear for dancers, skaters, and the theatre. Her enthusiasm for working with color and texture has led her to explore many types of embellishing techniques using twenty-first century tools. Her inspirations are seasonal color change, music, and dance. Elaine lives in Arlington, Texas.

Machine Techniques

Nancy Fiedler

When sewing machines were first mass-produced in the 1850s, they only created a lock stitch (straight stitch). Many special feet and attachments were designed to create special effects and finishes using that straight stitch. Accessories have evolved right along with the evolution of the sewing machine and today they lend themselves to every creative sewing technique one can imagine.

TIP: Check with your local sewing machine dealer to find the accessory that fits your sewing machine and creative needs.

Regardless of the machine brand and model and the accessory used, final sewing or quilting results can vary widely depending on fabric weight, thread weight, stabilizer, actual machine, and skill level. Always test the technique with the exact materials to be used in the project to ascertain the correct settings to get the desired effect.

As Janome educators who work daily with sewers and quilters like you, believe us, you can master these techniques. Just be sure to TEST-TEST-TEST.

These machine techniques are presented in alphabetical order; see the Index on page 63 to choose the project(s) that use them.

Fabric is assumed to be 40" wide for all projects in this book.
Seam allowance widths vary, so read the instructions carefully.

Binding

Binding the quilt is the finishing detail. To create a machine-applied double-fold binding, cut 2¼" strips crosswise from the binding fabric. Sew these into one continuous strip and then press the strip lengthwise wrong-sides together.

Sew the binding to the right side of the quilt, lining up the raw edges and mitering the corners. Press the binding to the back and pin in place. Stitch in the ditch from the top to secure the binding (see Ditch Stitching on page 9).

To create continuous bias binding, see page 15.

Another option is to use a quilt binding attachment that will sew the binding to the quilt in one step.

Cut the binding strips to the size recommended for the binding attachment, and sew the strips together for one long piece; make sure to allow 12"–18" extra length for starting and finishing.

Press the seams in one direction.

Cut the starting end of the strip at a 45-degree angle and then insert the angled end of the strip into the binding attachment with the wrong side facing the quilt edge.

Pull the binding under the presser foot about 4" so that the strip begins to form the fold. Starting at a corner, insert the quilt into the binding attachment, making sure the edge is tucked completely into the binding and under the presser foot. Sew at a medium speed.

To sew a mitered corner, stop stitching ¼" from the corner. Pull the quilt straight back about 3" and finger press the binding hems. Clip threads. Gently bring the quilt to the side of the machine and form the mitered corner on the front and back.

TIP: Use a quilt tack gun to hold the miters in place. First tack the back and then tack the front.

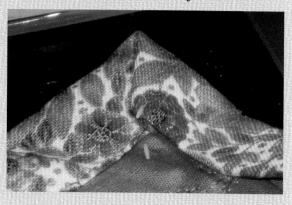

Carefully place the corner under the presser foot, and gently pull the binding back through the binding attachment until it is lying snugly in place. Sew the binding, making the next two corners in the same manner.

Stop sewing the binding about 2" from the end. Pull the binding to the back of the foot and cut it about 1" past the end. Cut the starting end of the binding even with the edge of the quilt. Hand form the bias corner covering the raw edge. Tack it in place with the quilt tack gun and then sew the binding in place.

To create an embellished binding, use Valora Hammond's method (see her project FRINGE FANTASY on page 31): Draw a diagonal line across the width of the binding fabric. Select a triple stretch stitch and stitch random rows of stitching using assorted thread colors. When all the embellishing is completed, cut the binding strips in the desired width; sew the strips together into one continuous strip and bind your quilt.

TIP: Try out other decorative stitches so that every binding is unique.

Buttonholes and Eyelets

(Editor's note: Eyelets are small openings designed for threads or cords to pass through. Buttonholes are shaped and sized to allow buttons of differing sizes to pass through. Both can be used as decorative details.)

Because the difficulty of creating a beautiful buttonhole on the machines we learned to sew on was often so discouraging, many of us have just given up or refused to go through the agony of making buttonholes.

But with new technology and state-of-the-art sewing machines, beautiful buttonholes and eyelets are easily within your grasp.

Every sewing machine manufacturer has a foot specially designed to create buttonholes. The foot or machine will allow you to correctly size the button. Be sure to follow the directions for the machine and always use a stabilizer on the wrong side of the fabric to prevent puckers. Test the buttonhole or eyelet on a stabilized scrap of the same fabric the project will be made from. If a more satin look is desired, shorten the stitch length.

Buttonholes don't have to be used for just buttons. Buttonholes for eyelets to weave 1" ribbon through are used in YIPES! STRIPES! on page 39.

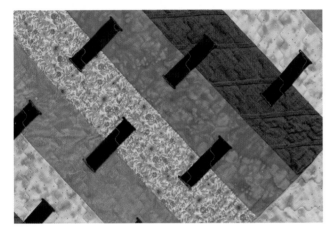

A tulle flower was created by weaving tulle ribbon in and out of machine-sewn eyelets on Kim Schultz's MONOCHROMATIC GLAMOUR pillow on page 59.

Circular Sewing

Circles can be simple to create with a circular sewing attachment. Check with your local sewing machine dealer to find the one compatible with your sewing machine.

Set the pivot point of the attachment for the radius (½ the diameter) of the circle.

Select the appropriate foot for the stitch chosen and be sure to place a stabilizer on the wrong side of the fabric to avoid puckers. Sew at a medium speed and watch as the circle automatically appears. See how Elaine Yingling used circular sewing on her TRIANGULAR PILLOWS on page 26.

Couching

Couching has been used in hand embroidery for centuries. It involves placing a thread or cord in position and then sewing over it with another thread to hold it in place. This is so easy with a sewing machine, a zigzag stitch, and a foot to hold the cord or ribbon in place! Experiment with decorative stitches for a unique look. Always test the stitch to make sure the stitch width and length are set so that the desired look is achieved.

A beading foot is ideal to hold cross-locked beads and heavy yarns and cords while sewing.

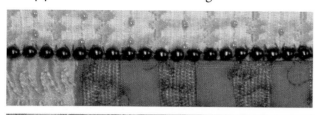

A multicording foot will hold several strands of cord in place while sewing. Select a stitch that will catch each cord, and, if necessary, adjust the stitch width and length to get the desired look.

A ribbon/sequin foot is ideal to hold ⅛" and ¼" ribbon in place. By selecting a decorative stitch and contrasting thread, the ribbon will be completely transformed.

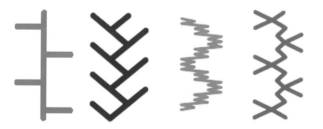

Assorted ribbon widths, thread and cord colors, and decorative stitches add lots of detail to the VICTORIAN ROMANCE pillow on page 44. Creator LuAnne Hartley suggests stacking the ribbon by using both of the guides on the foot. Place ¼" ribbon in the lower slot and ⅛" ribbon in the upper slot and couch them down.

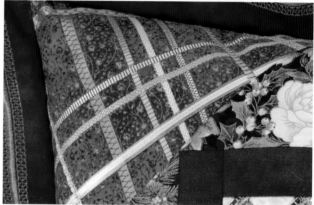

Decorative Stitch Quilting

Modern sewing machines give you the choice of many decorative stitches. These stitches can be a boon for those of us who are free-motion impaired! Attach the walking foot and select a stitch that moves in a forward motion to create interesting quilting effects with very little effort.

If you want to use an intricate decorative stitch that has a lot of forward and backward movement, first sew channels spaced approximately 1" apart using the walking foot and a straight stitch. Then sew the decorative stitch of your choice in the center of the channel using the satin stitch foot.

Ditch Stitching

Any time a seam needs to be secured, stitching in the ditch is a good option. To ditch stitch, place the fabric right side up under the presser foot so that the needle lines up with the seam. Then sewing at a medium-slow speed, sew on the seam line. Most often this is done with a straight stitch so that the stitches are hidden in the seam when it relaxes. A ditch stitch foot will help guide the stitching straight along the seam and keep the seam slightly open during the stitching process.

Good ditch stitching is not easy to see in photographs (or in person!), but it was used effectively in Fringe Fantasy (page 31), Triangular Pillows (page 26), and Twisted Ribbon (page 50). This photo of Fringe Fantasy shows a rare occasion of missing the ditch.

TIP: For those of us who miss the ditch, try using a decorative stitch. This can really be an eye-catching effect and it is most forgiving.

Embroidery

Twenty-first century technology allows us to become thread artists in a fraction of the time it took our hand-sewing grandmothers. Embroidery machines are now often a staple in the sewing studio.

For the best embroidery results, always:

Use the smallest hoop available that fits the selected design.

Use a stabilizer appropriate for the fabric and stitch density.

Seat the fabric and stabilizer securely in the hoop; don't shortcut with adhesive stabilizers and basting stitches. (Adhesive stabilizers should only be used for fabrics or items that cannot be secured in the hoop. Basting stitches are used to help hold the layers of fabric and stabilizer together.)

Press seams open if the design will be embroidered over a seam.

Lettering and appliqué are just the beginning of the design options available. Embroidery designs are available from many sources in all embroidery formats. Check with your local sewing machine dealer or online to find designs that will work for your project. Digitizing software is also a great way to create your own embroidery designs! Kim Schultz used embroidery to unexpected but great effect in Now I Know My ABCs on page 36.

Please remember: You purchase the right to use the embroidery design(s) personally. Ownership belongs to the designer, so do not share any purchased designs with your friends.

TIP: Create a signature label to put on all your quilts. Leave a space for the recipient's name and the date, which you can add with the machine's built-in lettering each time you make a quilt.

Free-motion Sewing

All domestic sewing machines have feed dogs. These pull the fabric under the needle to form the stitches. When they are in the up or engaged position, the sewing machine is in control! By dropping the feed dogs, or on some machines covering them, you can have complete control of the movement of the fabric. This allows free-motion sewing.

To sew raw edge appliqué using Louis Carney's method (see his project, MAGNIFICENT MANTELS, on page 47), place the first layer of fussy-cut elements on the background fabric in the desired positions. A light mist of temporary spray adhesive will hold them in place.

Set the machine for free-motion sewing. For the most part, this will mean a straight stitch with the feed dogs lowered or covered. Place SewSlip™ on the base of the machine. This is a specially designed surface that allows fabrics and battings to glide easily while free-motion stitching. Attach an open-toe free-motion foot and switch to a #90 topstitch needle.

When free-motion stitching, you control the length of the stitches by your movement. The faster you move the fabric, the longer the stitches will be. The feed dogs will not carry the fabric to the next stitch position. Make sure you are in a comfortable sewing chair at the proper height. Your arms should be straight and perpendicular to the base of the sewing machine.

You may want to engage the needle-down position, if that is a feature available on your machine.

Louis finds that it is also helpful to use a knee lift to raise and lower the presser foot. If your machine has a start/stop button and a foot control, you may see more even stitches when using the button, and he highly recommends trying this.

Start with a small running stitch around the outer edges of the first layer of flowers and accents. This will secure these pieces in place and allow for interior decorative stitching later. Once the first layer is secure, continue adding layers until your central design is complete. Add the remaining elements as desired.

Depending on the fabric colors, you may want to change the color of thread in the top to coordinate with the piece you are quilting. Embellish the appliqués with interior stitches to enhance the designs.

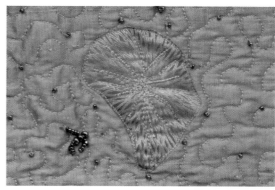

TIP: *You may want to switch to a very small 1.5mm zigzag to sew the interior stitching to add some variety.*

Stippling and meandering refer to a free-form loop design created to fill an area. Generally, the term "stipple" means the stitching lines do not cross and are close together; "meander" means the loops are medium-sized stitches with nice open curves.

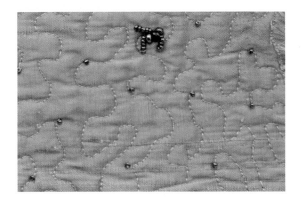

It is quite all right if the lines cross. Defined shapes such as the leaves Kathy Bond created on Front Door Welcome Quilt on page 19 are easily created with a little practice.

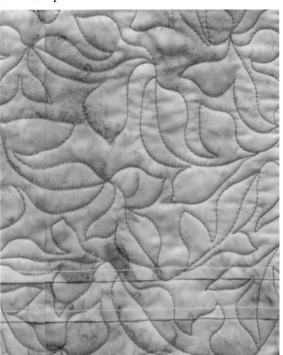

To make thread lace with Kathy Bond's method (see her Front Door Welcome Quilt on page 19), place a fabric square to be embellished right-side up on a flat surface with a piece of medium-weight water-soluble stabilizer fused to the wrong side.

Dribble assorted ribbons, yarns, and threads all over the surface.

Place a piece of water-soluble stabilizer over the entire piece.

Baste through all the layers to hold them securely together.

Thread the machine with embroidery thread. Attach the free-motion foot, select the straight stitch, and drop the feed dogs.

Using a pattern of large loops that cross over themselves many times, sew over the stabilizer, tacking down all the cording and threads trapped between the fabric and stabilizer.

When finished stitching, run warm water over the top and bottom of the square until the stabilizer is no longer visible; then soak the square in a bowl of warm water for an hour to remove the last of the stabilizer.

Rinse one more time, then pat dry with towels and lay flat to dry completely.

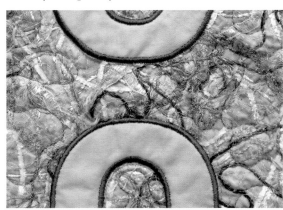

Fringing

Many years ago when sewing was more about garment construction than sewing for relaxation, feet (attachments) were designed to make many tasks easier. A foot was designed with a high bar in the center to make it easy to create tailor tacks. But when creative thinkers started working with it, they discovered it was the perfect foot to make fringe!

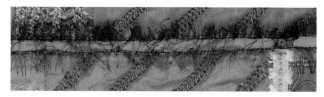

To make looped fringe, thread the needle and bobbin thread with the same color. Select the zigzag stitch and adjust the width to 2-2.5mm and the length to .35-.4mm.

To make cut fringe, select the overcast stitch and set the stitch width to 5mm and the stitch length to .4mm. After sewing the first line of fringe, lay the fabric on a flat surface. Cut the needle thread close to the fabric on the right-hand side of the stitching. After cutting the top thread, turn the fabric to the wrong side and use a stiletto to loosen the threads. Then use your fingers to fluff the fringe on the right side.

Sew multiple rows of looped or cut fringe side by side to fill an entire area. See ELEGANT STITCHES on page 56 for several uses of fringing.

Pintucks

Pintucks are often seen in garments, but several of the designers in this book have come up with some very clever pintuck details to add to their quilting projects. Look at the projects on pages 19, 26, 36, 39, 44, and 59 for the amazing design variety pintucks offer.

Corded Pintucks

Attach a pintuck foot and insert a 2mm twin needle or a twin needle that most closely fits the size of the channels in the foot.

Attach the pintuck cord guide, or if one is not available for the machine, tape a 2" length cut from a cocktail straw to the center of the needle plate in front of the foot. Insert a fine cord such as perle cotton into the guide (straw).

Thread the needles and bobbin with the same thread. Select the straight stitch. Tighten the needle tension to 7-8 to force the fabric to pucker.

Sew the first pintuck.

To make adjacent rows, move the fabric to the right or left of center, place the first pintuck into the next channel on the foot, insert the cord, and sew the second pintuck. Continue sewing in this manner to get the desired effect.

Diamond Pintucks

(Kim Shultz's method; see her MONOCHROMATIC GLAMOUR pillow on page 59.)

Draw lines spaced 1" across the width of the fabric.

On each mark, fold the fabric wrong-sides together and stitch, using the ¼" foot to form ¼" tucks.

Attach the all-purpose foot and the quilting guide bar set at 1" from the needle.

Starting in the center of the fabric, place the first two pintucks under the presser foot so that the folds touch each other. Continue to sew in the same way across the fabric.

Line up the first row of stitches with the quilting guide bar.

The quilting guide bar should glide over the seam just sewn. While sewing this seam, using the stiletto, lay the tucks in the opposite direction as the last time. Diamonds will begin to form.

Once this seam is sewn, turn the fabric around and sew 1" away from the center on the other side, laying

the tucks in the opposite direction. Continue in this manner across the length of the fabric.

Folded Pintucks

After determining the spacing of the pintucks, fold and press each one.

Attach an adjustable blind hem foot, or for ¼" pintucks, the ¼" foot.

Set the machine for a straight stitch and sew the length of the fabric using the guide of the foot to make an even line of stitching.

Press the pintucks in the desired direction.

Pleated Pintucks

Kathy Bond's method; see her FRONT DOOR WELCOME QUILT on page 19.)

Across the width of the fabric draw lines spaced ½" apart.

Insert the 4mm twin needle in the machine. Using the 2mm beading foot, select a straight stitch with center needle position and adjust the needle tension to the highest setting.

Beginning in the center of the fabric, stitch down each drawn line to create mock pleats.

Do not press this piece once the stitching is complete.

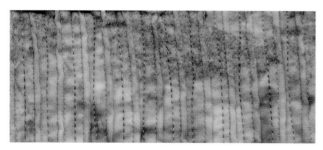

Wavy Pintucks

(Kim Schultz's method; see her NOW I KNOW MY ABCs project on page 36.)

Using the quilting guide bar set at 1" from the needle, sew a straight line across the width of the fabric. Move the fabric so that the quilting guide bar is resting on the first line of stitches and sew the next line. Continue in this manner to the end. Put in a DVD or favorite CD to listen to; this takes a little time but the results are worth it.

Attach the overedge foot. On each line that you made in the above step, fold the fabric wrong-sides together.

Stitch across using an overedge stitch. This is going to create some fun texture. Continue across the whole strip.

Sew along one edge of the strip a little less than ¼" from the edge so that it will be hidden in the seam allowance. Lay the tucks down toward you. Continue to the end.

Keep the bar at 1". Turn the strip around and sew the tucks down in the opposite direction of the first side. This will ensure that the tucks are lying in the correct position. Let the quilting guide bar glide along the sewn ¼" stitching line. Let the machine do the work; it will lay the tucks down as you go. Sew the length of the fabric.

Turn the fabric around and sew in the opposite direction. This time the tucks are going to lie down in the opposite direction creating a "wave" look.

 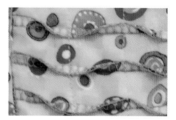

Piping

Adding piping between seams is an ideal way to add a tiny bit of color and texture. Piping was used to frame the blocks of the FRONT DOOR WELCOME QUILT on page 19 and to add more stripes to YIPES! STRIPES! on page 39.

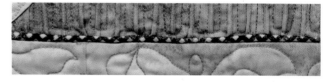

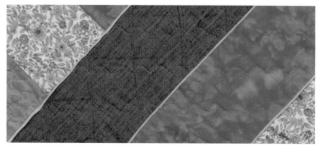

Attach a piping foot, or, to make mini piping, the pintuck foot. A zipper foot can also be used if the cord is too large to fit in the groove of the piping foot.

Set the machine for a straight stitch.

Wrap a bias strip around the cord and place it under the foot. See the sidebar on making continuous bias strips .

Sew the length of the bias strip encasing the cord.

Use the piping foot when sewing the piping to the fabric.

Reverse Bobbin Work

An interesting way to add decorative detail is reverse bobbin work. This technique allows the use of threads that cannot be threaded through the needle.

Nancy Fiedler's method uses all types of thread—perle cotton, fine yarns, YLI® Designer 6®, silk ribbon—any type of thread that will not go through the sewing machine needle.

Continuous Bias Strips

1. Cut a square of fabric.

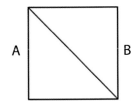

2. Cut on the diagonal line.

3. Use a ¼" seam. Sew side A to side B right sides together.

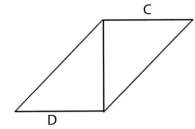

4. Open fabric and press seam.

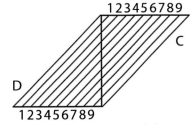

5. Draw lines spaced desired distance apart. Number each line at both ends.

6. Bring line C to D right sides together matching line 1 to 2, 2 to 3, 3 to 4, etc. Sew a ¼" seam.

7. Cut the tube on the marked lines to create a bias strip.

To prepare the fabric, fuse a fusible knit interfacing or a light-weight fusible web stabilizer on the wrong side of the fabric.

To set up the machine, wind the bobbin with the selected decorative thread. Thread the needle with embroidery thread that matches the embellishing thread. Another option would be to use a high quality monofilament thread.

For a very loose and textured look, place the bobbin in the bobbin holder/case and bypass the tension slot. For some brands of machines you may have to purchase a separate bobbin holder/case and loosen the tension screw all the way so that the thread can be placed in the tension slot.

For a more controlled look, use a separate bobbin holder/case and loosen the tension screw just enough so that the embellishing thread flows smoothly.

Bring the thread to the top of the needle plate.

Attach the satin stitch foot and select a decorative stitch; do not use satin stitches. Place the fabric right-side down on the machine. Lower and raise the needle once and pull the decorative thread to the top of the fabric so that the tail will be on the wrong side. Sew the stitch at a medium-slow speed.

Rolled Hem

A fast way to make tiny hems is to use the rolled hem foot. This foot is recognizable by the curl found on its toe.

After attaching the foot to the machine, make a tiny double fold at the edge of the fabric and then place the fold under the foot. Take one or two stitches to hold it in place and set the needle in the down position. Gently pull the fabric into the curl of the foot. Start sewing at a slow-medium speed and guide the fabric into the curl of the foot.

> *TIP: Hold the thread tails at the beginning of the hem to help ease the start of the hem through the foot. This foot takes a little practice, so be patient.*

Ruffles

Attach the ruffler to the machine making sure the C-clamp is correctly seated around the needle clamp screw. Set the machine for straight stitch.

Locate the ratchet gear feed plate, which is the lever on the face of the ruffler with the numbers marked

1 - 6 - 12. Set the plate at 1 to make a tiny gather with every stitch.

Locate the depth adjust screw (refer to the guide sheet provided with the ruffler) and set the screw to adjust the fullness of the gathers.

Place the strip of fabric over the bottom plate of the ruffler and under the plate that slides backward and forward.

Sew the length of the fabric strip at a slow speed.

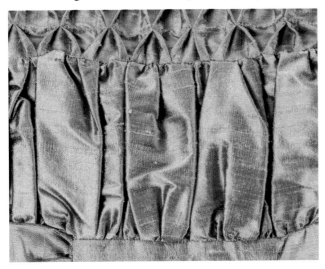

Smocking

(Elaine Yingling's method; see her TRIANGULAR PILLOWS on page 26.)

Fold the strip of fabric to be smocked in the center and press.

Set the machine for straight stitch, loosen the thread tension, and lengthen the stitch to 5mm. Using the straight stitch foot, baste one line on the marked center starting and stopping ½" from each end; then sew two more lines approximately ½" on left and right of the center starting and stopping ½" from each end. Gently pull up the basting threads to the desired ruffle length. Select an embroidery thread to contrast with the print and find a smocking stitch to sew over the basting threads of the ruffle.

Samples of Stitches for Smocking

Twin Needle Stitching

When zigzag machines became available the twin needle was born. This fun accessory has two needles on one shank. It comes in widths of 1.6mm to 6mm. Twin needles are used to make pintucks, create parallel lines of straight stitches, and as Elaine Yingling has used them for decorative stitching.

Note: Only use the 1.6mm or 2mm wide twin needles for decorative stitches.

To thread a twin needle, place two spools of thread on the spool holders so that the threads pull off in opposite directions. This helps to avoid tangles. Put the two threads together to thread the machine and stop at the needle. Place one thread in the right-hand needle thread guide and then the right-hand needle. Place the second thread in the left-hand needle thread guide and then the left-hand needle.

If the machine has a twin needle guard setting, turn it on. This will help prevent breaking the needle by selecting an inappropriate stitch. If the machine does not have a guard, be sure to turn the hand wheel and walk the needle stitch by stitch through the entire decorative stitch sequence to make sure the needle does not hit the presser foot or throat plate.

Select the stitch, attach the appropriate foot, and sew.

Quilting Guide Bar

Many walking feet come with a quilting guide bar. This is the perfect tool to create channel quilting without marking the fabric. Simply attach the bar to the foot and set it the desired distance from the needle. After sewing the first line of quilting, move the fabric so that the bar is on this line of stitches. Sew the next line using the bar as your guide. Continue on in this manner across the entire area to be quilted. It is a good idea to check the distance of the bar after sewing a couple of rows to make sure the channels stay consistent.

The first Janome educators book, **Creative Sewing Techniques by Machine** (AQS, 2010), has even more ideas to use in your sewing and quilting projects.

Front Door Welcome Quilt

17½" x 39½"
Designed and sewn by Kathy Bond

This door quilt is the perfect project to help build free-motion skills. Simple piecing gives the quilt visual movement; pintucks and pleats add some texture. Use the embroidery machine for perfect appliquéd letters and then drop the feed dogs and experiment with free-motion designs to quilt it all together.

Fabric

1 fat quarter of leaf print
½ yard of pink batik
1 fat quarter of cream batik
1 fat quarter of mottled dark green/brown print
⅝ yard of medium green batik
1 fat quarter of light green solid
1 fat quarter of small brown check
½ yard of brown batik
¾ yard of floral print (backing)
22" x 44" cotton low loft batting

Supplies

1¾ yards of ⅛" cotton cording
2½ yards of ¼" cotton cording
6 to 8 pieces 1 yard each of a variety of decorative cording and/or thick threads
1 square 12" x 12" and 7 squares 6" x 6" of water-soluble topping/ stabilizer
1 square 14" x 14" of medium-weight water-soluble stabilizer
7 hoop-size pieces of medium-weight tear-away stabilizer
Machine embroidery designs for applique letters–4" size
40-wt. rayon thread for embroidery
40- or 30-wt. decorative thread
4mm twin needle

Machine Accessories

¼" foot
Free-motion foot
Beading foot
Piping or zipper foot
5" embroidery hoop to fit embroidery machine

Cutting

Leaf print
1 rectangle 7½" x 10½"
1 rectangle 3½" x 10½"

Pink Batik
1 rectangle 11" x 18"
1 rectangle 9" x 14½"
1 square 12" x 12"

Cream batik
1 square 12" x 12"

Mottled dark green/brown print
1 square 12" x 12"
4 rectangles 3½" x 4½"

Medium green batik
1 rectangle 12" x 36"
3 rectangles 5" x 5½"
3 rectangles 5½" x 10"

Light green solid
7 squares 5" x 5"

Brown small check
1 pieced bias strip 1½" x 60"

Brown batik
2 strips 2" x 42"
3 strips 2¼" x width of fabric (WOF)

Floral print
1 rectangle 23" x 45"

Instructions

Thread Lace Square

Center the 12" pink batik square on the 14" square of medium-weight water-soluble stabilizer.

Setting aside 3 pieces of decorative cording to be used later, dribble the remaining cords and threads over the surface of the pink square, keeping the ends of the cords at the edges of the square. Place the 12" water-soluble stabilizer over the top of the square and pin securely all around the outer edges. Make the thread lace (see page 11).

Once completely dry, trim the square to 10½". Set this aside.

Pintuck Pleated Quarter-square Triangles

Place the 12" x 36" medium green rectangle on a flat surface. Starting at one of the 12" sides, mark 12" vertical lines every ½" across the entire 36" length with a chalk pencil.

Insert a 4mm twin needle in the machine and make pintuck pleats on each line (see page 14).

Do not press this piece once the stitching is finished.

Cut two 12" squares out of the rectangle and then cut both of the squares in half diagonally twice, creating quarter-square triangles.

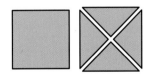

Quarter-square Triangle Blocks

Place the 12" cream batik square on top of the 12" mottled dark green/brown print square and align the edges carefully.

Cut the squares in half diagonally twice as you did with the pintuck square.

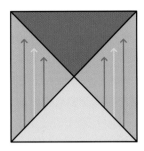

Using the quarter-square triangles you have created, lay out 2 blocks in this fashion. Be careful that the pintucks run in the direction of the arrows.

Being very careful not to stretch the pintuck triangles, sew the blocks together as they are laid out.

Being extra careful to keep the center of the block in the center, trim both blocks to 10½" square.

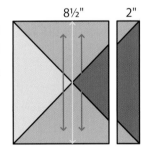

Create one final quarter-square triangle block in this fashion, again being careful to align the pintucks with the directional arrows.

First, trim this block to a 10½" square (again paying close attention to keeping the center true).

Then, on the side of the square with the dark green/brown triangle, trim off an additional 2".

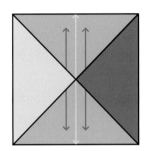

Pleated Pink Sections

Pink Block #1

To create the upper right pleated section of the wall quilt, place the 11" x 18" pink rectangle on a flat surface and mark four chalk lines spaced 1" apart.

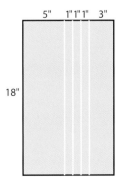

Front Door Welcome Quilt

With wrong sides together, create 4 pleats by folding on the drawn lines and pressing firmly.

Sew the pleats by placing each fold (fabric is still wrong-sides together), one at a time, under the presser foot and stitch ¼" from the fold all the way from the top of the rectangle to the bottom.

Press the pleats all in one direction, then press again in the opposite direction so the pleats stand erect.

Attach a beading foot to the machine in a size to hold the decorative threads or cords in place.

Thread the machine with thread that either matches the thread/cording or use monofilament thread.

Select the zigzag stitch and then narrow the width so that the stitch just covers the width of the thread/cord; slightly lengthen the stitch. Test on a scrap of pleated fabric to see if the embellishment is being sewn down in a pleasing fashion.

Lightly mark the rectangle with three flowing lines.

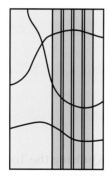

Starting with the line that crosses at the very top of the pleats, couch down the thread/cord on that line, pushing the pleats toward the left as you cross them.

Couch down the next line starting from the top and when you reach the pleats, push them to the right as you sew over them.

Finally, couch down the last thread/cord pushing the pleats once again to the left.

Trim the rectangle to 8½" x 17½", keeping the pleats in the right half of the block.

Pink Block #2
To create the lower right pink section of the quilt, mark the 14½" x 9" block with 3 lines.

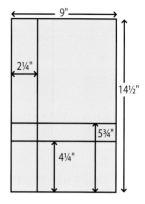

As before, fold the fabric wrong-sides together on each of the horizontal drawn lines and press firmly. Sew ¼" pleats and press toward the bottom of the rectangle.

Now fold wrong-sides together along the vertical line and press firmly, paying special attention to the area where the pleats cross each other. Sew this ¼" pleat, carefully managing the bulk at the intersections. Press to the right.

Trim the block to 8½" x 13½".

Assemble the Left Side of the Quilt
Lay out the blocks as shown in figure 8. Be sure that you have the correct quarter-square triangle blocks. The textured pintuck sections should have the tucks running vertically.

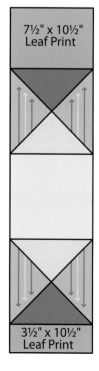

Create and Apply Thin Piping

Sew a 60" strip of bias brown small check fabric together by diagonally piecing the 1¼" strips from the fat quarter.

To create the piping, fold the strip over the ⅛" cotton cording. Using either a piping foot or a zipper foot, baste the strip around the cording. Don't stitch too close to the cord as this will not be the final stitching.

Use a tool like the Piping Hot Binding Tool to trim the seam allowance of the piping to ¼".

Place the piping down the right-hand side of the pieced quilt unit aligning the raw edges. Baste the piping down to the quilt unit but do not snug up the stitches close to the cording. Trim off leftover piping and save.

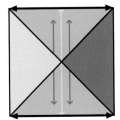

Place the remaining quarter-square triangle block on the table, and in the same manner as above, attach the piping to the two opposite sides (figure 9).

Assemble the Right Side of the Quilt

Lay out the blocks and sew them together with ¼" seams. You may need to use your zipper or cording foot to get the stitches snugged right up against the piping this time as you join the blocks (figure 10).

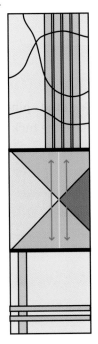

Now sew the two halves together referring to the quilt photo. Use your zipper foot or cording foot if necessary to get the stitches nice and snug against the piping.

Embroidery Machine Appliqué Lettering

Note: If you don't have an embroidery machine, cut out letters 4" high and appliqué them with a satin stitch.

Mark the center of the left side of the quilt and also lightly mark a vertical line 5" from the left raw edge top to bottom. This will be the centering line for the applique letters.

Based on the size of your letters, evenly space the center cross hair for each of the seven letters in "Welcome."

Place the marked fabric and tear-away stabilizer in the hoop in the position for the first letter. Place the water-soluble topping on top of the fabric.

Using the solid green 5" squares, appliqué the first letter.

Repeat for the rest of the letters. Remove all of the stabilizer when the embroidery is complete.

Quilting the Top

Layer the backing, batting, and top. Baste through all layers.

Kathy's choices for quilting:
Walking Foot - Quilt around each appliquéd letter.

Quilt a straight line between each row of pin tucks.

Free-motion – An overall leaf design is quilted in the lower right section. Sew over the pleats so that they are simply texture beneath the stitching.

For the top right section, quilt wavy lines parallel to the pleats.

Overlapping loops with thicker thread were quilted on the thread lace square.

The remaining areas were quilted with medium density meanders.

Once all the quilting is finished, baste around the outer edge of the top of the quilt approximately ⅛" from the raw edge. Do not trim the backing and batting.

Create Large Piping
Cut the ¼" cotton cording into two 45" lengths.

Using the brown batik 2" strips, wrap and stitch the cording inside the fabric with a basting length stitch and trim the seam allowance to ¼".

Baste the piping to the right and left side of the quilt top keeping the raw edges even. At the ends of the piping, pull the cording out a little ways from the fabric casing and trim so the cording ends just ¼" from the end of the quilt top.

Fold over the unstuffed ends of the piping fabric to the outside and pin in place.

Decorative Tabs and Functional Loops
Using the 4 mottled dark green/brown print 3½" x 4½" rectangles, fold them right-sides together. Use a ¼" seam to sew down the two opposite sides .

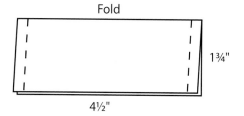

Turn right side out, push out the corners and press firmly. Of these 4, 2 will be bottom tabs; 2 will be top tabs.

Using the 3 medium green batik 5" x 5½" rectangles, fold them right-sides together and stitch ¼" seams down the opposite sides.

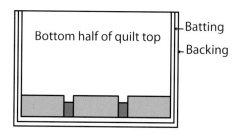

Turn right side out, push out the corners and press firmly. Use the quilt photo to arrange 3 medium green batik and 2 mottled dark green/brown print tabs on the bottom of the quilt.

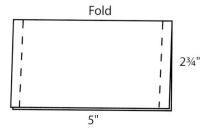

Baste all five tabs to the bottom of the quilt ⅛" from the raw edge.

Create the 3 loops for the top of the quilt using the remaining 3 medium green batik 5½" x 10" rectangles. Fold them right-sides together and stitch along the longest edge.

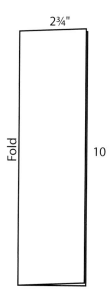

Turn right-side out and center the seam in the center of the long rectangle shape. Press.

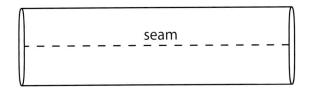

seam

Bringing the raw edge sides together, fold the rectangles in half again with the seam to the inside. This creates a loop that looks like the decorative tabs at the bottom of the quilt.

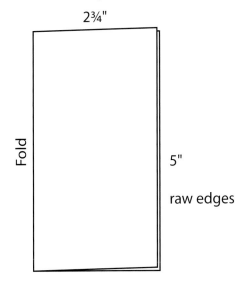

2¾"

Fold

5"

raw edges

Arrange the loops and tabs at the top of the quilt in the same manner as at the bottom of the quilt. Baste 1⅛" from raw edges.

Facing
Piece the 3 brown batik WOF strips with diagonal seams to create 1 long strip. Press the entire strip in half right-sides together.

Lay the raw edges of the strip along the raw edge of the quilt top. Leaving an 8" tail, begin sewing a ¼" seam to attach the facing to the quilt top. Use a zipper foot to get the seam snugged up to the piping along the sides of the quilt. Switch to a ¼" foot when you attach the facing along the bottom and top of the quilt. Join the facing with a diagonal seam when you get all the way around.

Check to see if the stitching is indeed snug against the side piping. If not, go back and stitch closer and tighter to the piping.

Trim the backing and batting even with the raw edges of the quilt and facing. Trim the quilt/batting/backing out of the corners.

Turn the facing to the back of the quilt, folding in the corners. Press securely.

Hand stitch in place.

Place a pole, rod, or stick through the loops and hang. Congratulations on finishing your FRONT DOOR WELCOME QUILT!

Small projects are ideal for practicing on free-motion skills. MORNING MIST on page 42 of *Creative Sewing Techniques by Machine (AQS, 2010)* introduces you to 3-dimensional motifs and more!

Triangular Pillows

18" x 25"

Designed and sewn by Elaine A. Yingling, Arlington, Texas

More Creative Sewing Techniques by Machine – Nancy Fiedler

Elaine discovered a fun frog print and a chrysanthemum fabric that became the inspiration for these accent pillows. In these instructions, substitute your fabrics for those Elaine chose for her frog pillows. In the photos, note that she altered some techniques for the chrysanthemum version, showing you how to unleash your creativity when you make your own editions of these clever pillows.

Fabric

½ yard striped frog print #1
½ yard allover frog print #2
¾ yard green stripe
¾ yard small-scale print
20" x 40" batting approximately ¼" thick

Supplies

Neutral color all-purpose thread
Assorted colors of machine embroidery thread
Perle cotton in contrast color
Paper-backed fusible web
Tear-away stabilizer
Polyester fiberfill for pillow
½ yard contrasting purchased piping
2 yards ⅛" wide woven ribbon
2 dragonfly buttons

Machine Accessories

¼" foot
Narrow (2mm) rolled hem foot
Adjustable blind hem foot
Satin stitch foot
Ditch stitch foot
Ribbon/sequin foot
Piping or zipper foot
Multicording foot
2mm twin needle
Quilting guide bar
Circular sewing attachment

Cutting

Ruffled Pillow

2 strips 4" x 18" striped frog print #1
2 strips 4" x 18" allover frog print #2
1 square 11½" x 11½" green stripe; cut the square twice on the diagonal for 4 triangles

 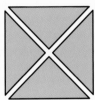

2 strips 3" x 31" green stripe
1 strip 4" x 2" small scale print
1 square 20" low loft batting

Appliqué Pillow

1 square 9" striped frog print #1; cut the square twice on the diagonal for 4 triangles

1 square 9" allover frog print #2; cut the square twice on the diagonal for 4 triangles

1 square 9" green stripe; cut once on the diagonal for 2 triangles

1 square 9" small print; cut once on the diagonal for 2 triangles

2 strips 4" x 40" small scale print

1 square 20" low loft batting

Triangular Pillows

Instructions

Use a ¼" seam unless otherwise directed.

Ruffled Pillow

Piecing

To piece pillow Side 1, sew 2 of the green-striped triangles along a short side of each triangle with the stripes mitered.

Cut the ends of the striped frog print #1 strips at a 45-degree angle. Sew the strips along the long side of 1 mitered triangle stopping ¼" from the top point; then join the 45-degree angled-ends at the top point for pillow Side 1.

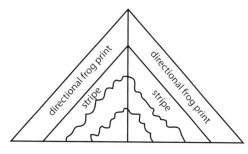

Repeat the previous steps with the allover frog print #2 strips to piece pillow Side 2.

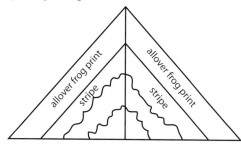

Press all seams open. Pin the triangles onto a layer of batting and cut to match the shape of the triangles.

Using the ditch stitch foot, ditch stitch the center mitered seams and connecting seams.

Enhancing Ruffled Pillow Side 1

Attach the satin stitch foot. Select an embroidery thread for the needle and a decorative stippling stitch. Sew 3 rows on the striped-print strip using the stripes as a guide.

Attach the rolled hem foot and hem all the sides of the 4" x 26" small-scale print strip.

Fold this strip lengthwise and press to mark its center. Gather the strip and add several rows of decorative smocking stitches. See page 17.

Pin the ruffle to the center seam. Select a different embroidery thread and add a row of smocking or hemstitching on both sides of the center row of stitches to secure the ruffle to the pillow.

Enhancing Ruffled Pillow Side 2

Select an embroidery thread for the machine needle. Change the foot to the satin stitch foot, select a decorative hemstitch, and sew over the seam connecting the frog print and triangle, pivoting at the mitered seam.

Select a different embroidery thread and decorative stitch. Attach the circular sewing attachment to the machine bed. Place the pivot point pin ½" from the edge of the seamed triangles. Sew 3 rows of different stitches at 2", 3", and 4" from the pin. Remove the circular attachment.

Choose an embroidery thread for the needle to match the ⅛" ribbon and attach the ribbon/sequin foot.

Select the zigzag stitch and adjust the width to 3.0mm. Couch the ribbon along a stripe about 1" from the connecting seam of the triangle, remembering to pivot at the mitered center seam.

Attach dragonfly buttons within the striped triangle by machine or by hand.

Ruffled Pillow Construction

Before joining the front and back to the sides, trim both triangles to measure 18" at the sides and 25" at the base.

Change the foot to the straight stitch foot and thread the machine with neutral color all-purpose thread. Sew the two 3" x 31" strips together at both ends with a ¼" seam. Press the seams open.

Right sides together, pin the center seam of the strip at the top point of Side 1. Pin and stitch a ½" seam with the second joining seam at center of the triangle's base.

Pin and stitch the pillow back to the panel, aligning the 3 corners, leaving 4–5" open to stuff the pillow. Trim the corners, turn and press the seams. Stuff the pillow and close the opening with hand stitches.

Appliqué Pillow

Appliqué Pillow Side 1

Sew the 4 allover print triangles on the short sides to form a square. Press seams open.

Change foot to zipper or piping foot and sew the contrast piping to 2 adjacent sides of the square with a ¼" seam.

Sew the 2 small-print triangles to the piping edges of the square, stitching just inside the first seam.

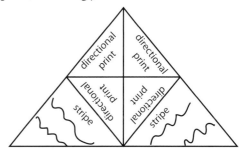

Pin a layer of batting toward the wrong side of the triangle and cut to match the triangular shape.

To quilt the allover pieced panel, insert the twin needle, then thread each needle with a different embroidery thread. Align the right needle in the ditch and stitch in the ditch on 1 of the pieced seams. Rotate the square 90 degrees and stitch in the ditch with the right needle. Rotate 90 degrees 2 more times so that you have stitched in the ditch 4 times with the right hand needle and have created 3 lines of stitching with a heavier, contrast thread coverage in the center.

Insert the standard needle and select a contrast embroidery thread. Starting at the outer edges of the small-print triangles, quilt parallel rows ½" apart until stitching to the triangle center.

Appliqué Pillow Side 2

Sew the 4 striped frog print triangles on the short sides to form a square. Press seams open.

Sew the 2 green-striped triangles to the square to create one larger triangle.

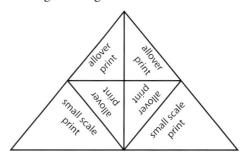

Triangular Pillows

Pin a layer of batting toward the wrong side of the triangle and cut to match the triangular shape.

Insert the twin needle and thread each needle with a different color embroidery thread. Select a feather stitch, and cover the crossed seams of the directional print triangles. Add an additional row to highlight the print.

Insert the single needle and attach the multicord foot. Feed 3 strands of perle cotton into the slots of the multicord foot with 2" extending behind the foot.

Select a contrast embroidery thread and a decorative stitch to couch the strands. Apply the trim to the connecting seams between the striped and printed triangles.

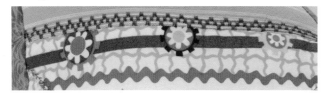

Following the manufacturer's directions, apply the paper-backed fusible to the wrong side of the allover frog print. Fussy cut 2 frog motifs to appliqué onto the striped triangles.

Place tear-away stabilizer behind the centered appliqués without sandwiching the batting. Attach the satin stitch foot, select the zigzag stitch; set the stitch width to 2.0mm and the stitch length to .40mm. Satin stitch around the outer edges of the frogs, then change thread color. Repeat the satin stitch to echo the appliqué shapes.

Appliquéd Pillow Construction

Before joining the front and back to the sides, trim both triangles to measure 18" at the sides and 25" at the base.

Using a fine chalk marker, draw lines 2" apart on the 2 strips 4" x 40". Press the strips at each line.

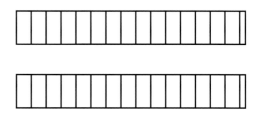

Attach an adjustable blind hem foot to help keep the stitching lines even. Thread the machine in a color to match the fabric and sew a straight stitch approximately $\frac{1}{16}$" from each fold to create the pintucks.

Sew the strips together, then cut the resulting strip 61½" long. Sew the ends together to form a continuous piece.

With right sides together, pin the side panel to the pillow front, centering a pintuck at the top of the triangle. Stitch together with a ½" seam.

Repeat the step connecting the pillow back with the side panel, aligning all corners. Leave 4–5" open for stuffing. Trim the corners, turn right side out and press the seams. Stuff the pillow and sew it closed with hand slip stitches. Finally, hand tack ribbon bows at opposite corners of the print square.

Now that you have tried the circular sewing attachment to add a simple detail to a pillow, learn how to create appliquéd and quilted circles with the COLLISION OF COLOR wallhanging on page 38 of *Creative Sewing Techniques by Machine* (AQS, 2010).

Fringe Fantasy
36" x 36"
Designed and sewn by Valora Hammond, Denver, Colorado

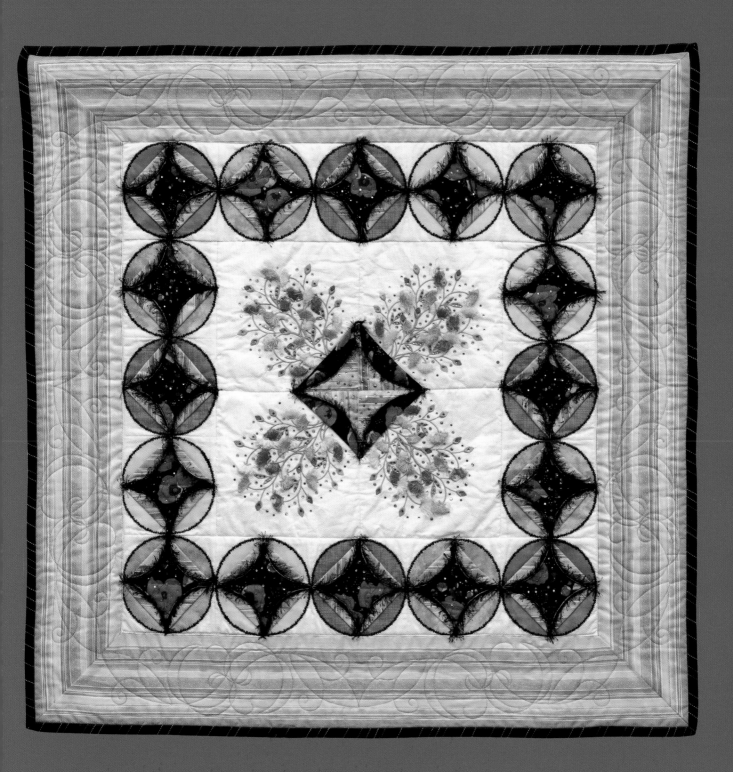

With this dimensional wallhanging, spring will always be in the air. Machine-embroidered fringe flowers burst out of the center cathedral window. Fringe also frames the edges of the cathedral windows in the border. The windows are simple to make using a circular sewing attachment.

Fabric
1 yard of white background fabric
1½ yards of striped fabric
¾ yard of coordinating print fabric
¼ yard or fat quarter of 5 different colored fabrics
    (i.e., blue, yellow, orange, green, pink)
1¼ yard of backing fabric
½ yard of binding fabric
45" x 45" batting

Supplies
Embroidery design: Flower C fringe AIHFF117
    from Adorable Ideas (see Sources on page 63)
Quilting motif embroidery design of choice
Assorted colors of embroidery thread
Cut-away stabilizer
Seam sealant
Iron-on tear-away stabilizer
Cotton thread
Monofilament thread
Heat-set crystals and applicator
Assorted beads

Machine Accessories
5" x 7" embroidery hoop to fit machine
Embroidery foot
All-purpose foot
Appliqué foot
Satin stitch foot
Circular sewing attachment
Fringe foot
¼" foot
Ditch stitching foot

Cutting
Background fabric
Cut 4 squares 10" by 10"
Cut 16 squares 6" x 6"; then mark the center
    point of each square

Striped fabric
Cut 4 strips 6" x 45" with the stripe running the
    length of the strip (borders)
Cut 4 pieces 4½" x 4½"
Cut 16 pieces 6" x 6"; then mark the center point
    of each square

**Coordinating print fabric
for cathedral windows**
Cut 1 square 8" x 8"
Cut 16 squares 6" x 6"; then mark the center
    point of each print square

Fabric for appliqué circles
Cut 2 squares 6" x 6" of blue and yellow
Cut 4 squares 6" x 6" of orange, green, and pink;
    then mark the center point of each square

Instructions

Embroidery

In the edit screen of the embroidery machine, open the Flower C fringe pattern. Copy and paste so there are 4 sections of flowers: 1 in the top middle, 2 angled on each side, and 1 last toward the bottom, overlapping all the stems. Resize as desired.

Note: Be sure to turn off the thread trimmers on the embroidery machine since the fringe flowers are a very wide satin stitch.

Stitch one combination of these clusters on each of the 10" squares using cut-away stabilizer.

Note: The use of a variegated thread would add interest to the fringe flowers. Alternatively, stop the machine after each flower for a thread change so each blossom is a different color.

Secure the back of the fringe flowers with seam sealant on the wrong side of the block where the flowers are attached to the stem.

Trim squares down to 8", including the cut-away stabilizer.

Sew the 4 sections together with the stems toward the center using ¼" seam allowance.

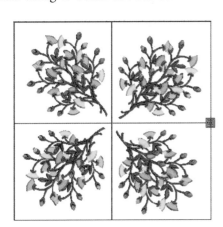

Cathedral Windows

Center Window

Sew the 4 striped 4½" squares together in a pinwheel fashion using ¼" seam allowance.

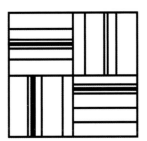

Back the 8" square of coordinating print with the iron-on tear-away stabilizer.

Using the circular sewing attachment and an all-purpose foot, center the 8" print square right-side up on the pin. Place the striped pinwheel face down with the middle of the pinwheel on the pin. Set the circular sewing attachment at a 3½" radius to make a 7" circle, select the straight stitch, and sew a circle.

Remove the fabric from the attachment and tear off the stabilizer. Cut out the circle a scant 1¼" from the stitching line.

Determine the center of the circle, and on the print side, slash the fabric about 1½" to create an opening to turn the circle right-side out. Turn and press.

Border Windows

Back the 16 coordinating print 6" squares with iron-on tear-away stabilizer.

Put the center of the first print square on the pin of the circular sewing attachment right-side up. Center a striped 6" square right-side down on the pin.

Stitch a 5" circle by setting the circular sewing attachment at 2½".

Remove the square from the attachment and then tear off the stabilizer. Cut out the circle a scant ¼" from the stitching line.

Slash the center of the striped fabric about 1½" following the middle stripe. Turn right-side out and press.

Make 16 border windows.

Fringing the Window Circles

Attach the fringe foot. Select the overcast stitch and change the settings to stitch length 1mm and stitch width to 7mm.

Stitch twice around very close to the edge of each circle.

Clip the bobbin thread to create the fringe.

Border Appliqué Circles

Apply the iron-on tear-away stabilizer to the back of the 16 white background squares (6" x 6").

Place the center of the first 6" background square right-side up on the pin of the circular sewing attachment. Center a colored appliqué 6" square right-side up on the pin of the circular sewing attachment.

Set the circular sewing attachment at 2½" so a 5" circle will be made.

Sew a straight stitch and stitch around the circle. Do not move the circular sewing attachment or remove the circle.

Use a pair of sharp scissors to trim the appliqué fabric close to the straight stitch.

Select a decorative stitch and finish the edge of the appliqué circle.

Trim each square down to 5½", leaving a ¼" seam allowance beyond the appliqué circles. Remove the iron-on tear-away stabilizer.

Make 16 appliquéd blocks.

Assembling the Quilt Top

Use ¼" seams.

Sew 2 strips of the appliquéd blocks using all five colors—pink, yellow, orange, green, and blue.

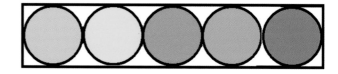

Sew two strips of the appliquéd blocks with three colors—yellow, orange, green.

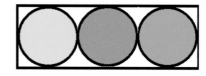

Press the seam allowances to one side.

Sew the three block strips to opposite sides of the embroidered block unit.

Sew the five block strips to the top and bottom of the embroidered block unit.

Striped Borders and Mitered Corners

Find the center of each border. Match with the center of the middle appliquéd block on each side of the quilt.

Sew the borders to each side. Stop ¼" from each end. Press the seam allowance toward the border.

To find the stitch line for a mitered corner, fold one border down with its right side to the right side of the quilt top. Have the other border folded out and flat.

Mark the angle from the stitch line of the folded down border to the corner where the two borders cross.

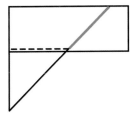

Fold the borders right-sides together, matching the seam ending points. Stitch along the line that was drawn to determine the angle of the miter.

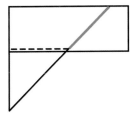

Trim the seam allowance to ¼" and then press open.

Putting It All Together

Sandwich the backing, batting, and the quilt top and baste through all layers.

Stitch in the ditch along each seam line, using monofilament thread to stabilize the quilt layers together, starting in the center and working toward the borders.

To create the cathedral window effect in the center block:

Place the 7" circle in the center embroidered unit.

Stitch from one side to the other in the center of the circle using the seam lines as stitching guides.

Sew the center of the circle going in the opposite direction.

Fold each free curved edge toward the center. Pin in place.

Stitch the curved edge down.

Repeat the process and sew a cathedral window in the center of each appliquéd circle in the border.

Quilting

Quilt the striped border as desired. Valora used the embroidery machine and quilted a motif in the hoop.

Sew on the binding. Valora created stitch-embellished binding (see page 31) for this quilt and then added beads, sequins, and crystals for the extra details that make this wallhanging worthy of a prime position.

> Three-dimensional effects add so much visual interest to quilting projects. See how Valora used 3-D techniques to create a CELTIC SUNRISE in *Creative Sewing Techniques by Machine* (AQS, 2010).

Now I Know My ABCs

54" x 65"

Designed and sewn by Kim Schultz, Slidell, Louisiana

This is an awesome and educational quilt for a lucky child. Let's use some cool techniques and have fun with this one. You will be using machine embroidery, free-motion quilting, and decorative stitching using the overedge foot.

Note: If you don't have an embroidery machine, no problem. Fussy cut squares from your favorite print fabric.

Fabric

1 yard white fabric for embroidery
1¾ yards yellow print for sashing
2 yards green print for the Square-in-a-Square block, outer border, and binding
60" x 70" batting
1¾ yards backing fabric

Supplies

Embroidery design: A Is For from Bunnycup Embroidery (see Resources)
Assorted colors of embroidery thread
Neutral color all-purpose thread
2 yards medium-weight tear-away stabilizer

Machine Accessories

4" embroidery hoop to fit the machine
Embroidery foot
¼" foot
Overedge foot
Walking foot with quilting guide bar
Free-motion foot

Cutting

White (or favorite print to fussy cut)
Cut 26 squares 6" x 6"

Yellow print
Cut 4 squares 4½" x 4½"
Cut 15 strips 3½" x width of fabric (WOF)

Green print
Cut 30 blocks 4½" x 4½"
Cut 6 strips from border fabric 5" x WOF
Cut 7 strips for binding 2¼" x WOF

Instructions

Note: Use ¼" seams

Embroidered Blocks

Embroider a design in the center of each 6" white square making sure to use the stabilizer during the embroidery process. Trim all embroidered blocks to 4½" square and remove the stabilizer. (If you don't have an embroidery machine, fussy cut 4½" squares from your favorite fabric.)

Layer the embroidered block and 1 of the green print blocks right-sides together.

Sew a ¼" seam around the perimeter of the block.

On the wrong side of the green fabric, mark across the block on the diagonal. With a scissors, carefully cut on the diagonal line to the seam lines, making sure you are ONLY cutting the print fabric and NOT

Opposite: Joseph photographed with his mom's permission.

the embroidered block. Press these corner triangles away from center.

Use the remaining 4 green print 4½" squares and the 4 yellow print 4½" squares to create the corner blocks. Place 1 green and 1 yellow square right-sides together.

Sew a 1¼" seam around the perimeter of the block.

On the wrong side of the green print fabric, mark across the block on the diagonal. With a scissors, carefully cut on the diagonal line to the seam lines, making sure you are ONLY cutting the green print fabric and NOT the yellow print. Press these corner triangles away from the center.

Wavy Pintuck Sashing

Sew the 15 yellow print sashing strips right-sides together forming 1 very long strip of fabric. Press seams open.

Thread the machine with a contrasting thread color and follow steps 1, 2, and 3 for Wavy Pintucks on page 14 to create tucks across the 3½" width of the sashing strip along its entire length. The waves will be completed during the quilting process.

Assembling the Quilt Top

Refer to the quilt photo for the layout.

Cut 36 pieces 5½" long from the sashing strip. Sew these to the right and left sides of each of the 30 blocks, creating 6 rows.

Cut 7 sashing strips, each 46" long. Sew these across the tops and bottoms of the block rows, attaching all rows together with sashing between them and at the top and bottom.

Final Border

Sew the 5" border strips together so that you have 2 pieces 54½" long. Sew these to the right and left sides of the quilt top.

Sew the 5" strips together so that you have 2 pieces that measure 65½" long. Sew these to the top and bottom of the quilt top.

Quilting

Layer the backing, batting, and top. Baste through all the layers.

Kim used free-motion quilting in all areas except the sashing.

To quilt the sashing, refer to page 14 (Machine Techniques, Wavy Pintucks). Attach the walking foot and the quilting guide bar. Set the bar at 1" Let the guide glide along the seam where the block is sewn to the sashing, sewing the tucks down in the opposite direction. Let the machine do the work; it will lay the tucks as you go. Sew the length of the sashing strip.

Do this to all of the sashing pieces.

Add the binding to the quilt using your favorite method.

Remember to label the quilt.

Kim has a talent for adding interesting texture to her quilts. See how she transformed solids into textures in BLACK, WHITE, AND RED ALL OVER on page 16 of *Creative Sewing Techniques by Machine* (AQS, 2010).

Yipes! Stripes!

Approximately 60" x 90"
Designed and sewn by Nancy Fiedler, Dwight, Illinois

Fabric

1¼ yards green cotton for stripes

1¼ yards light blue mini print for stripes

2 yards hot pink cotton batik for stripes and middle border

2¼ yards blue cotton batik for stripes and outside border

2 yards multicolor print for stripes and binding

1¼ yards gold cotton batik for piping and inside border

5½ yards coordinating striped cotton print for backing

3 yards 90" wide batting

Supplies

18 yards ¹⁄₁₆" cording for piping

8 yards 1½" wide green rickrack

9 yards 1" wide black grosgrain ribbon

Neutral color all-purpose thread for piecing

Variegated thread in colors to coordinate with fabrics for quilting

Machine Accessories

New size 12 sewing machine needle

Pintuck foot

Pintuck cord guide

2mm twin needle

¼" foot

Buttonhole foot

Walking or evenfeed foot

Fabric Preparation

Prewash all the fabrics, dry them, and press out wrinkles.

Create Texture with Pintucks

Set up the sewing machine to create corded pintucks.

Cutting

Important Note: Create green pintucked cotton before cutting.

From the green pintucked cotton, light blue mini print, hot pink batik, blue batik, and multi color print cut 1 strip 21" by the width of the fabric (40") of each color.

Cut 20 rectangles 4" x 21" from each strip.

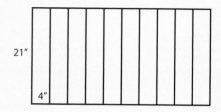

From the green pintucked cotton, light blue mini print, hot pink batik, blue batik, and multicolor print; cut 4 strips 4" x the width of the fabric (40") of each color.

Set the remaining hot pink, blue, and multiprint fabrics aside to be cut for borders and binding after the top is pieced and measured. (Note: There will be leftover striped pieces. Use these to create coordinating pillows or as a starting point for bright-colored tote bags or purses.)

From the gold fabric cut 1 square 26". Set the remaining fabric aside to be cut for a border.

On the green cotton, use a fabric marker and draw a line at a 45-degree angle across the length. Sew a corded pintuck on this line (see page 12).

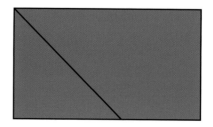

Move the fabric so that the first row of stitches lies in the first channel to the left of the center and sew another pintuck.

Move the fabric so that the pintucks lay in the two channels to the left of the center and sew a third pintuck.

Continue sewing triple rows of corded pintucks spaced 2" apart across the entire width of the green fabric.

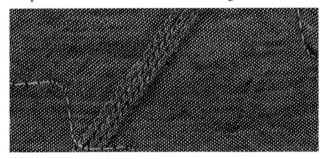

Make Piping

Cut the 26" gold square in half on the diagonal. Make a 1" wide continuous bias strip following the directions on page 15.

Set up the machine to make mini piping with the pintuck foot, the ⅟₁₆" cording, and the continuous bias strip. Once it is made, trim the insertion seam to ¼".

Piecing the Top

Following the color arrangement below, sew 25 of the 21" strips together to form a panel approximately 21" x 87½". Square up the long edges so that the panel measures 19" x 87½".

Draw lines at a 45-degree angle from the upper right hand corner and the lower left hand corner.

Cut on these lines. Set the 2 short ends aside for another project; they will not be used in this quilt.

Sew the remaining 25 strips together to form another 21" x 87½" panel. Set this panel aside; this will be cut into the corners later.

Sew 2 green pintuck strips 4" x 40" right-sides together to create a 4" x 80" strip.

Continue making 4" x 80" strips of each of the 5 colors. There will be two 80" strips of each color.

Sew the 1½" wide green rickrack along both sides of the pink strips. Center the rickrack along the raw edge and sew a scant ¼" from the edge.

Sew the mini piping along 1 side of the green, multicolor print, and the light blue mini print strips.

Sew 5 strips together. Make two.

Sew the mini piping to the side of each panel that does not have piping.

Yipes! Stripes!

Sew the 5 colored strips to the diagonally cut panel.

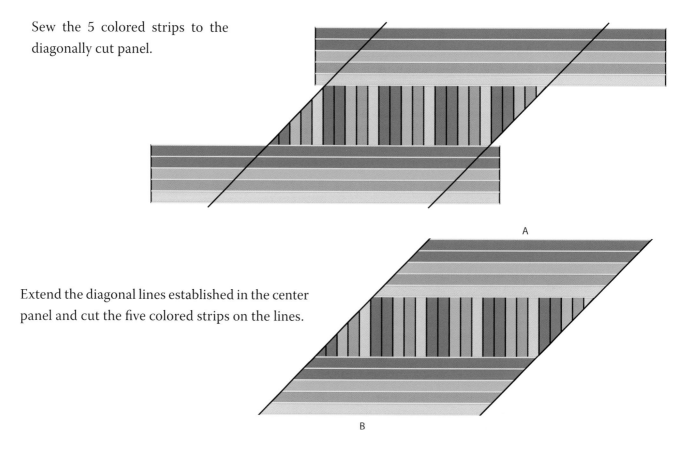

Extend the diagonal lines established in the center panel and cut the five colored strips on the lines.

Measure sides A and B. If necessary, square up all sides so they are even.

Place the remaining 21" x 81½" multicolored panel on a flat surface. Cut 2 corner pieces using the measurements from the previous step.

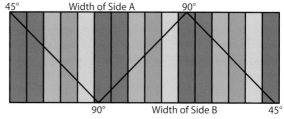

Sew the corners to sides A and B.

Rotate the quilt top so that it is a rectangle; if necessary, square up all 4 sides.

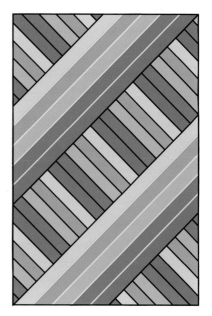

Woven Ribbon

Make 1" buttonholes in the center of each 4" x 19" colored strip spacing the rows of buttonholes 4" apart.

Carefully cut each buttonhole open.

Weave the black ribbon through the buttonholes to add extra movement to the quilt top.

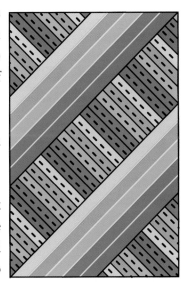

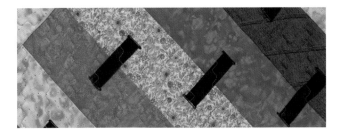

Baste the ribbon ends at the edges.

Adding the Borders

From the gold batik cut 8 strips 1½" by the width of the fabric for the inside border.

From the hot pink batik cut 8 strips 2½" by the width of the fabric for the middle border.

From the blue batik cut 8 strips 3½" by the width of the fabric for the outside border.

Measure the length and width of the pieced top. Using these measurements, piece the border strips and cut them to the lengths needed. Sew the borders to the quilt top panel.

Quilting

Piece the backing as needed to fit the quilt top.

Sandwich the top, batting, and backing; baste through all three layers.

Select a serpentine stitch and quilt the stripes of each panel in the opposite direction.

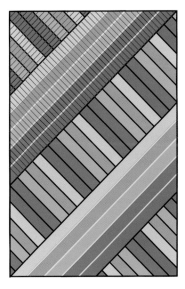

Stitch in the ditch between each border.

Quilt the borders with built-in decorative stitches.

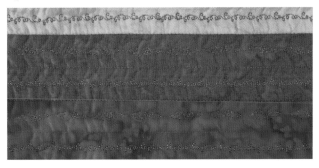

Add a label to the finished quilt.

Binding

Cut 8 crosswise strips of the multicolor print fabric in the width desired for the binding. In the quilt shown the strips were cut 2" for the quilt binding attachment (see page 5).

Sew the binding to the quilt in your preferred method.

Nancy loves to quilt with built-in decorative stitches. In her quilt BIRDS IN PARADISE on page 34 of *Creative Sewing Techniques by Machine* (AQS, 2010), use of these stitches creates a subtle texture.

Victorian Romance
16" x 16" (without flange)
Designed and sewn by LuAnne Hartley, Welcome, North Carolina

Heirloom sewing techniques do not need to be limited to children's wear and elegant blouses. LuAnne used several to add texture and details to printed cotton to create a pillow that will work perfectly in her home.

Fabric

⅓ yard cream print for center block

¼ yard deep red for inner frame and flange

¾ yard floral print for inner corners and pillow back

⅓ yard gold print for outside corners

⅓ yard green print for outside corners

Supplies

½ yard tear-away stabilizer

Assorted colors perle cotton for couching

Approximately 8 yards small cording for pintucks

Assorted colors embroidery threads

Cotton thread for piecing

5 yards ribbon in assorted sizes ¼"–⅛"

Fiberfill stuffing

Hand sewing needle

Machine Accessories

Multicording foot

Pintuck foot

½" foot

Ribbon/sequin foot

Open toe satin stitch foot

Ditch stitch foot

Cutting

Cream print

1 square 10" cream print for center block

Dark red

2 strips ½" x 6½" to frame center block

2 strips 1½" x 8½" to frame center block

2 strips 2¾" x 16½" for flange

2 strips 2¾" x 20¾" for flange

Floral print

2 squares 6⅝" for inner corner

Gold

1 square 10" for outside corners

Green

1 square 10" for outside corners

Backing

1 square 20¾" x 20¾"

Embellishment for Center Block

Draw diagonal lines 1" apart on the 10" cream square. Lay a piece of tear-away stabilizer behind the square.

Attach the multicording foot and thread the machine with a contrasting thread.

Place 2 strands of cord in the left and right guides of the multicording foot. Select an appropriate stitch and couch the cord on the drawn lines.

Trim the square to 6½".

Pillow Top Construction

Use ¼" seam allowances.

Sew a 1½" x 6½" strip to each side of the center square.

Sew a 1½" x 8½" strip to the top and bottom of the center square.

Cut the two 6⅝" x 6⅝" print squares in half on the diagonal. Sew these pieces to all sides of the center square block.

Place a piece of tear-away stabilizer on the wrong side of the 10" green square. Using the ribbon/sequin foot, couch the ribbons randomly with different decorative stitches.

Trim the square to 8⅞" x 8⅞" and cut it in half on the diagonal. Sew the triangles to 2 opposite sides of the square.

Create corded pintucks on the 10" gold square. Space the pintucks apart or stack them side by side.

Trim the square to 8⅞" x 8⅞" and cut it in half on the diagonal. Sew the triangles to the two remaining sides of the square.

Outside Flange

Sew the 2 strips 2¾" x 16½" to opposite sides of the pillow top.

Next sew the 2 strips 2¾" x 20¾" to the top and bottom of the pillow top. Draw a line down the middle of all sides of the flange for placement of the first decorative stitch.

Embellish the pillow flange with decorative stitches of your choice.

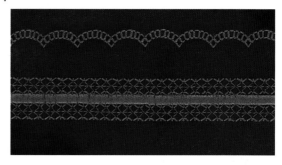

Assembling the Pillow

Lay the backing fabric on top of the pillow front with right sides together. Sew around the entire edge leaving about 3" open for turning and stuffing. Turn the pillow right-side out.

To create the flange, use the ditch stitch foot and a straight stitch to sew around the entire pillow, stitching in the ditch between the pillow flange and pillow top. Leave about 3" open in the same location as the previous step for stuffing the pillow.

Stuff the pillow with fiberfill or any type of pillow stuffing you prefer. Close the flange opening by stitching in the ditch with the ditch stitch foot. Hand sew the outside edge closed.

If you like the elegance of this project, follow the directions for Quilted Centerpiece on page 24 of *Creative Sewing Techniques by Machine* (AQS, 2010) to make a coordinating table centerpiece.

Magnificent Mantels!

14" x 50" (without fringe)
Designed and sewn by Louis Carney, New York, New York

Glorious, gorgeous, and simply divine! Create this inviting, decorative mantel quilt to add elegance to any décor. Raw edge appliqué and free-motion meandering are the techniques used to embellish this stunning accessory.

Silk dupioni is the base and a large cotton floral is the focal fabric. You will also need some accent fabrics with some interesting details for the appliqué.

Fabric

(Adjust yardage according to your mantel measurements)

2 yards of silk dupioni

1 yard large floral print

¼ yard each of assorted companion prints

½ yard of 90" wide cotton batting

1 yard medium-weight tear-away stabilizer

Supplies

Rayon or cotton threads to coordinate

Metallic threads

Beaded trim to coordinate: Purchase one length of the finished piece plus 6"

Decorative corded trim: Purchase the finished length plus 2 x the finished width plus 9"

Spray sizing

Temporary spray adhesive

Newsprint or other paper for pattern

Beads or heat set crystals and applicator

Machine Accessories

¼" foot

Open toe foot

Zipper foot

Open toe free-motion foot

Size 90 topstitch needles

Size 80 Microtex needles

SewSlip™ surface

Preparation

Measure the width and length of the mantel; add any additional length for drop. If the mantel is curved, trace the actual shape on newsprint for a pattern.

Note: Before cutting, be sure to add ¼" seam allowance to each side of each piece.

Cut a top and back from the silk dupioni according to the measurements or pattern. Fussy cut large flowers and other shapes from the print fabrics.

Use the sizing to stabilize the silk top and back.

Starting in the center, lay the large fussy-cut flowers in a pleasing arrangement. Layer these with scrolls, leaves, and some of the smaller flower pieces. It is a good idea to pin these in place first and rearrange as necessary.

Once these are acceptable, use the temporary spray adhesive to hold them in place. Work in small sections and add the layers as you go. You'll want to keep in mind that these pieces are layered and some will overlap others.

Attach the batting to the back of the top using the temporary spray adhesive.

Place a piece of tear-away stabilizer under each appliqué using the temporary spray adhesive to hold the stabilizer in place.

Use free-motion raw edge applique to attach the pieces to the fabric (see page 10 from Machine Techniques).

Attach the zipper foot to the sewing machine and set the machine back to normal sewing. Wind a bobbin out of the cotton thread to match the back fabric. Thread the machine with the cotton thread.

Attach the purchased trim and cord using the zipper foot for close accuracy. You may need to move your needle position to stitch close to the trim/cording.

TIP: Clip the trim/cord when turning corners or sewing around a curve so that the trim will lay flat.

Sew the top and back sections right-sides together. Don't forget to leave a 3" opening in the back area, to turn inside out.

TIP: Sew with the top facing up, then sew on the previous stitching lines.

Turn the mantel quilt inside out, remembering to clip corners and curves first. Press. Stitch the opening closed.

Set the machine for free-motion sewing. Thread the needle with embroidery or metallic thread and matching cotton thread in the bobbin.

Quilt an open meandering stitch in any open areas on the top.

Outline the appliqués to add more depth and dimension to your quilt.

Once you've added as much or as little quilting to your piece, give a good press to set the stitches.

Add crystals or beads to make this mantel quilt sparkle!

If free-motion sewing is not your bag, take a look at how Louis used a twin needle to quilt his FIT FOR A KING/QUEEN BED SCARF on page 60 of *Creative Sewing Techniques by Machine* (AQS, 2010).

Twisted Ribbon

29" x 66"
Designed and sewn by Valora Hammond, Denver, Colorado

This versatile piece can be used as a wallhanging or as a table runner, and it can also serve as a queen-size headboard. The truly ambitious could adapt it as the drop border design for a bed quilt. The center motifs are machine embroidered, and all the twists are embellished with built-in decorative stitches, which add loads of details.

Note: A queen size headboard will need 12 blocks, a full will need 10 blocks, and a king size will need 16 blocks. Fabric allotment is for queen size.

Fabric
½ yard of fabric for Twist 1
½ yard of fabric for Twist 2
¾ yard of background fabric
2 yards of striped fabric for borders
2 yards of backing
½ yard for binding
36" x 72" of batting
12 yards each of 10mm ribbon in two colors

Supplies
Embroidery design: DigiBobbE®:
    Collection 4, Bubbles and Pearls
Cotton thread for piecing
Decorative threads for reverse bobbin work
Embroidery thread
Iron-on tear-away stabilizer
Heat-set crystals and applicator

Machine Accessories
5" x 7" embroidery hoop to fit machine
Embroidery foot
Bobbin case for reverse bobbin work
¼" foot
Satin stitch foot
Even feed foot
Beading foot
Ditch stitch foot
5" x 7" embroidery hoop

Cutting
Background fabric
24 squares 3½" x 3½"
30 squares 4½" x 4½"
6 squares 6" x 6"; cut twice diagonally to yield 24
    quarter-square triangles.

Twist 1 and 2 fabrics
24 pieces 4½" x 4½"
3 pieces 6" x 6"; cut twice diagonally to yield 12
    quarter-square triangles of each color.
6 pieces 5" x 5"; cut once diagonally to yield 12
    half-square triangles.

Twist 1 fabric
4 pieces 3¼" x 3¼"

Stripe border
2 strips 6" or width of repeat x 72"
4 strips 6" or width of repeat x 18"

Construction

Blocks

Draw a diagonal line from corner to corner on one 4½" square of twist 1 fabric. Place it on top of a 4½" square of twist 2 fabric right-sides together. Stitch ¼" on each side of the drawn line. Cut between the stitches. Press the seam open. This will create the center square for 2 blocks.

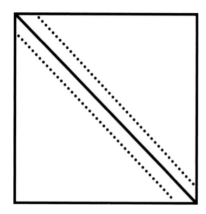

Draw a line from corner to corner on a 4½" background square. Place the background square and twist 1 color square right-sides together. Stitch ¼" on each side of the drawn line. Cut on the diagonal line between the stitching. Press the seam open. This will create two corners.

Repeat this step with the twist 2 color to create another pair of corners.

Sew 1 small background quarter-square triangle and 1 quarter-square triangle of a twist color together to form a half-square triangle. Press seam open.

Take 1 half-square triangle of the other twist color and sew it to the 2-color triangle.

Make a set of each color combination.

Trim all squares to 3½".

Assemble the block according to Figure 2. Press all seams open.

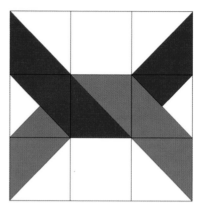

Sew the blocks into units; join the units to make the center (block piece).

Borders

On the 18" long strips of striped fabric place the 3 ¼" square in the corner. Stitch diagonally across the square.

Trim the seam allowance to ¼". Press open. Join the two 18" pieces together.

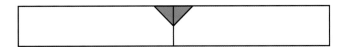

Attach the shorter border, matching its center to the center of the block piece. Stop sewing ¼" from the edge of the block piece.

Attach the longer border, stopping ¼" from the edge of the block piece. Press the seam allowance to the border.

To mark the miter for the corners, leave one border laid out flat and fold the other border so that the right sides are together. Mark from the stitching line to the point where the two borders cross.

Fold the borders right-sides together, matching the stitching line of the borders. Sew along the line that was determined for the miter. Trim the seam allowance to ¼".

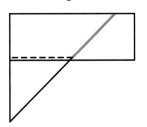

Embroidered Reverse Bobbin Work

Set the machine up for embroidery using the embroidery foot.

Bring in the oval design in the format for the machine.

Wind a bobbin very slowly with the thicker decorative thread/cord.

Do a test sample to make sure the bobbin case has loose enough tension. If necessary, adjust the tension on the spare bobbin case.

Fuse the iron-on stabilizer to the back of the center of the quilt top.

Find the center of the background area (formed when two blocks are sewn together) and mark on the wrong side by pushing a pin through the quilt top and marking on the stabilizer.

Hoop the quilt top with the wrong side facing up in the hoop and centering the mark in the center of the hoop.

Embroider a motif on all of the available spaces.

Leave long tails of the decorative thread/cord to bury later into the quilt.

Decorative Stitching on Twists

Decorate the ribbon twists of the quilt top by doing reverse bobbin work (see page 15) with an open decorative stitch in the middle of each of the twisted ribbons.

Then, using embroidery thread and a different decorative stitch, add a row of stitching on both sides of the reverse bobbin work.

Finishing the Quilt

Layer the backing, batting, and top. Baste through all the layers.

Stitch in the ditch using the ditch stitching foot on all the seam lines, then quilt as desired.

Valora used reverse bobbin work and a straight stitch in a wavy line to quilt the borders and then couched over beaded trims along the twists.

Bind the quilt as desired.

Twisted Ribbon Edging

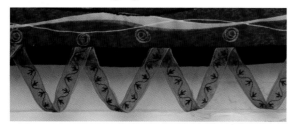

Stack the two ribbons together and place them under the satin stitch foot. Select a decorative stitch and sew down the middle of the ribbon the entire length.

TIP: If the ribbon is hard to work with, make it easier to stitch on by dissolving water-soluble stabilizer scraps in a small amount of warm water and then paint the ribbon. Allow to dry. This will help the ribbon to stick together and make it easy to work with.

Wind the decorated ribbon into a ball.

Mark every 2" on the binding of the quilt.

Set the machine up for a straight stitch. The ribbon will be attached by stitching in the ditch along the binding.

Lay the ball of ribbon on the quilt with the end toward the binding and the ball to the left of the presser foot. Stitch over the ribbon end.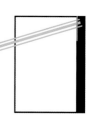

Pass the ball behind the presser foot and to the right stopping at the 1½" mark on the needle plate.

Tip: If the machine does not have this mark, place a piece of painters tape 1½" from the needle on the bed of the machine.

Fold the ribbon toward the foot making a 1½" loop. Bring the ribbon back to the left side in front of the foot at the next 2" marking. Stitch the ribbon down.

Pass the ribbon behind the foot and bring it out to 1½" fold, and then bring it to the left to stitch the ribbon down.

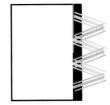

Continue in this manner adding loops to all 4 sides.

Add crystals where desired.

Attach a decorative curtain rod to the wall and thread the rod through the twisted outside ribbon to hang above the bed as a headboard, or sew a sleeve on the back if you wish to hide the rod.

If you like to use unusual edge finishes for your projects, see the two-color prairie points on TWILIGHT GARDENS on page 57 of *Creative Sewing Techniques by Machine* (AQS, 2010).

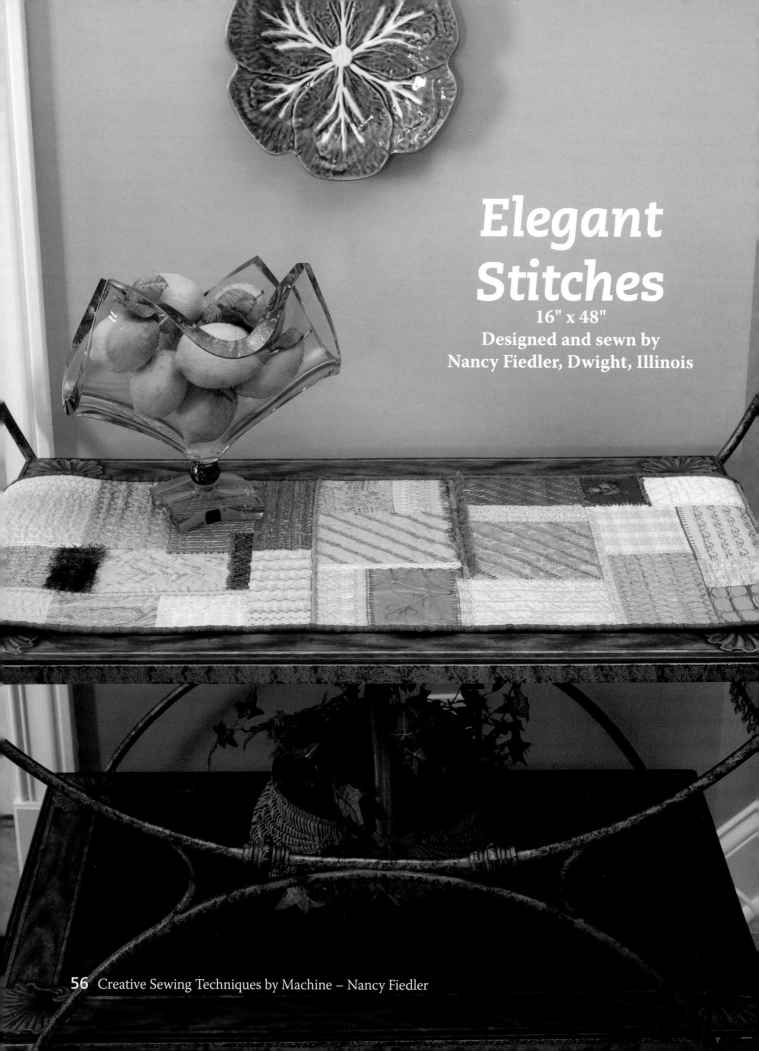

Elegant Stitches

16" x 48"
Designed and sewn by
Nancy Fiedler, Dwight, Illinois

Randomly placed scraps of silk are foundation pieced to create a background to showcase multiple decorative stitches and embellishing techniques. The elegance of the silk belies the ease of creating a one of a kind table runner like this one.

Fabric

¾ to 1 yard scraps of silk in assorted colors and sizes
20" x 52" muslin for foundation (approximate)
20" x 52" batting
20" x 52" cotton backing
⅓ yard 40" wide silk for binding

Supplies

Assorted yarns or unspun polyester/rayon threads
    for couching and reverse bobbin work
Assorted ribbons
Assorted cross-locked beads and cords for couching
Assorted embroidery threads for decorative stitching
    and fringe

Neutral color all-purpose sewing thread
Assorted loose beads
1 yard beaded fringe
Double-sided wash-away basting tape
Size 70/11 needles

Machine Accessories

Satin stitch foot
Beading foot
Ribbon/sequin foot
Fringe foot
Even feed foot

Instructions

With a permanent fabric marking pen, draw lines on the muslin foundation to indicate the approximate size of the finished table runner (16" x 48").

Thread the sewing machine with a neutral color thread and new size 70/11 needle.

Starting at any corner, place down a scrap of silk right-side up. Overlap the drawn lines slightly, and stitching close to the raw edges, sew the scrap to the foundation.

Select another piece of silk. If necessary cut the scrap to the size you desire. Place the new scrap right-side to right-side of the previously sewn piece, lining up a raw edge. Sew an approximate ¼" seam. Flip the new piece right-side out and press it in place.

Continue adding assorted pieces of silk to cover the table runner between the drawn lines.

Sometimes you may want to add a piece that does not quite fit in a corner or overlaps an existing piece. Fold under the raw edge and finger press. Then place a strip of the wash-away basting tape on the folded edge and press the edge in place. The decorative stitching will secure the seam later.

When all piecing is completed, sandwich the backing, batting, and top and baste well through all the layers.

Elegant Stitches

Attach the walking foot and stitch in the ditch in all of the seams.

Now the fun begins. Examine the fabrics and your embellishing assortment. Some silk pieces may only require decorative stitch quilting. Cover unsightly seams by couching ribbon, cords or beads. Add extra dimension with reverse bobbin work. Add lots of detail, as this is what this project is all about!

After all the embellishing is completed, square up the edges of the table runner.

Bind the table runner as desired. Double-fold binding was used for this tablerunner.

Hand sew loose beads, or add crystals for even more eye-catching details.

Finish the table runner with beaded fringe at each end.

Fringe can be so much fun to make, see how Nancy used it to add texture to the FRINGED JOURNAL project on page 76 of *Creative Sewing Techniques by Machine* (AQS, 2010).

Monochromatic Glamour

21" x 21"
Designed and sewn by Kim Schultz, Slidell, Louisiana

I love pillows because they allow me to try new techniques without committing my resources to a large project. This pillow is so fun to make! You will experiment with different techniques and materials that you will fall in love with and be able to incorporate in future adventures. Embellishment with eyelets, texture with gathers, and diamond tucks will make this an eye-catching accent pillow.

Fabric

1½ yards silk dupioni

2 yards 5½" wide tulle ribbon

2¾ yards beaded fringe

5" square lightweight fusible cut-away stabilizer

21" pillow form

Supplies

Yarn needle

Stiletto

Thread to match fabric

Machine Accessories

Ruffler (a gathering foot would also work)

¼" foot

All-purpose foot

Quilting guide bar

Cutting

6 strips 5" x width of fabric

1 rectangle 22" x 20"

1 rectangle 22" x 15"

1 square 5" x 5"

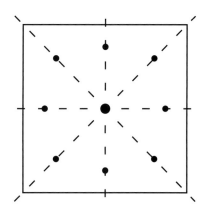

Instructions

All seams are ½".

Center Round

To create eyelet placement, find the center of the 5" square by lightly marking its diagonals. Lightly mark the vertical and horizontal centers. Mark the center. Mark ¾" in from the edge on the vertical and horizontal lines. Mark 1" in from the edge on the diagonals.

Using a stabilizer behind the fabric, make the eyelets at these marks using the built-in eyelet stitch or very small buttonhole.

Thread the yarn needle with the tulle ribbon. Insert the ribbon in any eyelet except the center from the back. Pull through, leaving a tail about 4" long on the wrong side of the fabric.

Insert the needle down through the center eyelet from the front to the back, pulling the ribbon loosely. Insert the needle up through the opposite eyelet and then down through the center eyelet, always pulling ribbon loosely. Continue doing this until all eyelets are used. Work with the ribbon to arrange it so that it looks like a flower. When you have an arrangement that is pleasing to you, tack the ends down on the back of the fabric to hold the ribbon in place. Put this piece aside.

Gathered Round

Note: If you don't have a ruffler attachment, you can still do this the "old-fashioned" way by sewing a basting stitch down the length of the long ends and gathering by hand, adjusting the gathers so that they are even. A gathering foot also works great for this project.

Using 2 of the 5" x width of fabric strips, seam the 2 pieces at the short ends to create a strip 5" by about 80". Using the ruffler, gather both sides of the long edges.

Cut 2 pieces of the gathered strip into 5" lengths. Sew these to 2 sides of the embellished 5" square.

Cut 2 pieces from the long gathered piece, each 13" long. Sew these to the other sides of the center piece, forming a new 13" square.

Diamond Pintuck Round

Sew the remaining 4 strips 5" by width of fabric together forming 1 long strip, 5" by about 160".

Mark every inch across the short width of the strip.

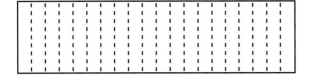

Follow the steps on page 13 to make diamond pintucks on this strip.

From the long strip of diamond pintucks, cut 2 pieces 13" long. Sew these on 2 opposite sides of the square.

From the long strip of diamond tucks, cut 2 pieces 22" long. Sew these to the long sides.

The square is now 22". Baste the beaded fringe to the pillow front, matching the edge of the fringe to the edge of the fabric with the beads facing the center of the pillow.

Pillow Back

Make a double 1½" hem on the 22" edge of the 15" piece. Set aside.

Make a double ½" hem on the 22" edge of the 20" piece. On this hem, select a decorative stitch built into the machine.

Assembling the Pillow

Layer the fabrics in this order:

Pillow front, right side up (make sure beads are all inside seam line).

The larger pillow back piece, right side down, raw edges even with pillow front.

The smaller pillow back piece, right side down, raw edges even with pillow front.

Sew all 4 sides with a ½" seam. Sew first with a longer stitch length, flip right-side out and make sure the fringe looks OK. Once you have the fringe perfect, stitch again with a normal stitch length.

Clip the corners and turn the pillow right side out.

Get ready; once your friends see this pillow, everyone will want one!

If you enjoy the fine look of silk dupioni, make a companion pillow like the SIMPLY AUTUMN project on page 46 of *Creative Sewing Techniques by Machine* (AQS, 2010) a a springboard for your imagination.

Sources

Adorable Ideas
http://www.adorableideas.com

Applique Letters
http://fancyfontsembroidery.com

Bunnycup Embroidery™
http://www.bunnycup.com

DigiBobbE®
http://www.bonniemccaffery.com

Piping Hot Binding Tool
http://www.piecesbewithyou.com

Sew Slip™
http://sewslip.com

Silk Scrap Packs by Delectable Mountain Cloth
http://www.delectablemountain.com

Index: Projects by Technique

More AQS Books

This is only a small selection of the books available from the American Quilter's Society. AQS books are known worldwide for timely topics, clear writing, beautiful color photos, and accurate illustrations and patterns. The following books are available from your local bookseller, quilt shop, or public library.

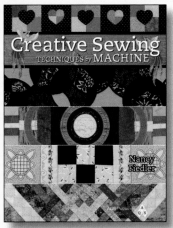

#8235 $24.95

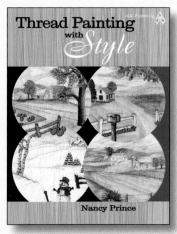

#8354 $28.95

#8529 $26.95

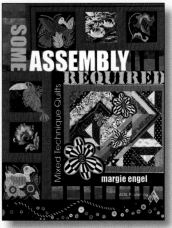

#8531 $26.95

#8662 $26.95

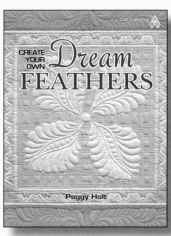

#8670 $26.95

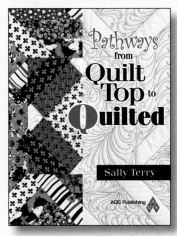

#8348 $28.95

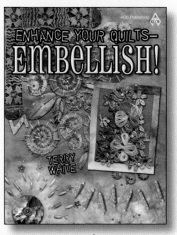

#8532 $26.95

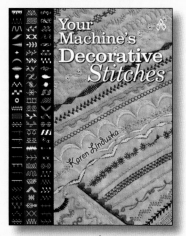

#8353 $24.95